THIS BOOK BELONGS TO

Name: Age:

Favourite player:

2017/2018

My Predictions...   Actual...

The Blues' final position:

The Blues' top scorer:

Championship Winners:

Championship top scorer:

FA Cup Winners:

EFL Cup Winners:

Contributors: Paul Macro, Peter Rogers & Rob Mason

A TWOCAN PUBLICATION

©2017. Published by twocan under licence from Ipswich Town FC.

ISBN 978-1-911502-02-9

PICTURE CREDITS: Dan Sakal & Warren Page, Grant Pringle, Action Images, Press Association.

£9

DeanGerken

1
GOALKEEPER

COUNTRY: England DOB: 22/05/1985

Gerken joined Blues back in July 2013 after impressing while on trial with the club and signed a new two-year contract this summer. He played five times throughout the 2016/17 campaign, and will again challenge Bartosz Bialkowski to be Mick McCarthy's first-choice goalkeeper this season.

DominicIorfa

2
DEFENDER

COUNTRY: England DOB: 24/06/1995

A versatile defender, Iorfa joined Town on-loan for the 2017/18 campaign from Wolverhampton Wanderers. He can play either right-back or centre-back and played in Aidy Boothroyd's England U21 side that made it to the European Championship semi-finals last summer!

JonasKnudsen

3
DEFENDER

COUNTRY: Denmark DOB: 16/09/1992

Knudsen joined Ipswich Town on a three-year deal in 2015, keeping him at the club until 2018. A Danish left-back, well known for his long throw-in, he instantly established himself as a regular on the pitch.

Luke Chambers

4 DEFENDER

COUNTRY: England **DOB:** 28/09/1985

Club captain, Chambers joined Town on a free transfer, after his contract at Nottingham Forest had expired back in July 2012. He impressed in his debut season, being named Town's Players' Player of the year and signed a two-year contract extension at the end of the 2016/17 campaign.

Tommy Smith

5 DEFENDER

COUNTRY: New Zealand **DOB:** 31/03/1990

Smith progressed through the Academy ranks at the club and is now performing for the first team at the heart of defence. He suffered a frustrating campaign in 2016/17, after undergoing back surgery in September, but recovered to play for the All Whites at the Confederations Cup.

Adam Webster

6 DEFENDER

COUNTRY: England **DOB:** 04/01/1995

The ball playing defender will be hoping to establish himself at the heart of Towns' defence after missing a large part of the 2016/17 season through injury. His versatility has been highlighted by Mick McCarthy as an important part of his game with Webster capable of playing at either right-back or centre-back.

Teddy Bishop

7 MIDFIELDER

COUNTRY: England **DOB:** 15/07/1996

An Academy scholar who has progressed right through to the first team, since joining Town as an eight year-old. Offering great composure and an eye for a killer pass the tenacious midfielder will be hoping to push on and cement his place in Mick McCarthy's squad again this term.

MartynWaghorn

9
FORWARD

COUNTRY: England **DOB:** 23/01/1990

Ipswich Town fought off tough competition to sign Waghorn on a two-year contract in August 2017. He adds firepower to the Blues' front line and scored the winning goal on his league debut, in a 2-1 victory over Barnsley.

ColeSkuse

8
MIDFIELDER

COUNTRY: England **DOB:** 29/03/1986

Skuse joined Town in 2013 from Bristol City, where he had spent his entire career. He has played an integral part in the Blues first team since signing and 2017/18 is his fifth season with Blues.

David McGoldrick

10
FORWARD

COUNTRY: Republic of Ireland **DOB:** 29/11/1987

McGoldrick completed a permanent move to Ipswich in 2013 after originally joining on loan from Nottingham Forest. He ended his first full season at Town as top scorer with 16 goals but has struggled with injury over the past few seasons. When fit, he is a regular in Mick McCarthy's side.

BersantCelina

11
MIDFIELDER

COUNTRY: Kosovo **DOB:** 09/09/1996

A tricky, attacking midfielder, Celina signed on loan for the 2017/18 campaign from Manchester City. It will be his first proper taste of English football having only appeared for City on a handful of occasions. He did, however, appear regularly while on loan with Eredivisie side, FC Twente last term, scoring five times.

JordanSpence

12
DEFENDER

COUNTRY: England **DOB:** 24/05/1990

Spence can either play at right-back or at centre-back. He initially penned a six-month deal keeping him at Portman Road until the summer of 2017 having been without a club since being released by MK Dons at the end of the previous campaign, but signed a new two year contract at the end of last season.

JoeGarner

14
FORWARD

COUNTRY: England **DOB:** 12/04/1988

Garner signed a three-year deal prior to the beginning of the 2017/18 campaign having joined from Rangers for an undisclosed fee. He has history against Town, namely scoring a hat-trick for Preston at Deepdale in an FA Cup tie back in 2014.

TomAdeyemi

15
MIDFIELDER

COUNTRY: England **DOB:** 24/10/1991

A midfielder with a real eye for goal, Adeyemi penned a two-year deal in July 2017. He spent the 2016/17 season on loan at Rotherham from Cardiff City where he scored seven times in all competitions.

Callum Connolly

16
DEFENDER

COUNTRY: England   DOB: 23/09/1997

Connolly signed up at Town on a season-long loan from Everton on August 2017 deadline day. He can play anywhere across the back four and spent the latter part of the 2016/17 season at Wigan Athletic, scoring a brace on his debut.

Danny Rowe

17
MIDFIELDER

COUNTRY: England   DOB: 09/03/1992

Brave, strong and good on the ball, Rowe joined Town on a three-and-a-half year deal in January 2017 from National League side Macclesfield Town. He made his debut on 18th March 2017 away to Cardiff City, coming on as a substitute.

Grant Ward

18
MIDFIELDER

COUNTRY: England   DOB: 05/12/1994

Ward can play anywhere across the midfield and, as shown early on, has a real eye for goal. He joined Town in August 2016 and firmly established himself as a valued member of the first team in his first season with the Club.

Luke Hyam
19 MIDFIELDER

COUNTRY: England **DOB:** 24/10/1991

Hyam adds energy and tenacity to the Town midfield and is often deployed just in front of the defence, breaking up opposition attacks. He has had a difficult two seasons with injury and is under contract until 2018.

Freddie Sears
20 FORWARD

COUNTRY: England **DOB:** 27/11/1989

Sears signed with Town back in January 2015, and has since firmly cemented himself into the first team. He scored seven league goals last season, including a brace in the vital win against Wigan in April.

Flynn Downes
21 MIDFIELDER

COUNTRY: England **DOB:** 20/01/1999

Downes signed a new three-year deal in the summer of 2017, keeping him at Portman Road until 2020. Mick McCarthy has high hopes for him after impressive displays in pre-season and Downes will be looking to secure himself a place in the Blues starting 11 this season.

Tristan Nydam
22 MIDFIELDER

COUNTRY: England **DOB:** 06/11/1999

A product of the Blues Academy, Nydam signed his first professional contract with the Blues in November 2016. He made his full debut in August 2017 in the 2-0 victory over Luton in the League Cup. He also received a call-up, along with Flynn Downes for the England U19 squad in the summer of 2017.

11

IPSWICH TOWN
FOOTBALL CLUB

Andre Dozzell

23 MIDFIELDER

COUNTRY: England **DOB:** 02/05/1999

A product of Town's academy, Dozzell made his debut at just 16 years old, scoring a header in a 1-1 draw with Sheffield Wednesday in April 2016. Unfortunately, he tore his cruciate ligament during the opening game of the 2017/18 season and was ruled out for the rest of the season.

Michael Crowe

24 GOALKEEPER

COUNTRY: Wales **DOB:** 13/11/1995

Town's number three stopper, behind Bartosz Bialkowski and Dean Gerken, Crowe has impressed since arriving in Ipswich. He has spent time on loan with Woking, Stevenage and Braintree whilst at Portman Road, as he looked to gain exposure to first-team action.

Myles Kenlock

30 DEFENDER

COUNTRY: England **DOB:** 26/11/1996

Kenlock joined in 2014 as a scholar, he made his full debut in the Capital One Cup win over Stevenage in August 2015 and was singled out for praise by the boss. Since then he has gone on to be a key part of the first-team picture at Portman Road, signing a new two-year deal in 2017.

Bartosz **Bialkowski**

33
GOALKEEPER

COUNTRY: Poland **DOB:** 06/07/1987

Town's No 1 keeper, Bialkowski played in all but two of Blues' league games last season. He won both the Supporters' Player of the Year and the Junior Blues Player of the Year for his efforts in 2016/17.

Ben **Folami**

34
FORWARD

COUNTRY: Australia **DOB:** 08/06/1999

The young striker has impressed for the Under-23 squad and made his debut for the first team at the start of the 2017/18 season.

Ben **Morris**

35
FORWARD

COUNTRY: England **DOB:** 06/07/1999

Having gained international caps at Under-17 and Under-18 youth level the talented striker joined Woking on loan during the 2016/17 season. He made his first team debut for Town on the 22nd August 2017 against Crystal Palace in the Carabao Cup.

Monty **Patterson**

36
FORWARD

COUNTRY: New Zealand **DOB:** 09/12/1996

Patterson made his first team debut at the start of the 2017/18 season having spent part of the previous season on loan at Braintree Town. He currently has 13 full international caps for New Zealand, scoring 1 goal.

13

Adam **McDonnell** 37
MIDFIELDER

COUNTRY: Republic of Ireland   DOB: 14/05/1997

McDonnell joined Town from Shelbourne in 2014. Having made a handful of first team appearances he is currently on loan to Aldershot Town with the hope of gaining further first team experience.

Pat **Webber** 38
DEFENDER

COUNTRY: England   DOB: 14/03/1999

Webber signed a two year scholarship deal in July 2016 and was another youngster to be handed his first team debut against Crystal Palace in the Carabao Cup at the start of the 2017/18 season.

Luke **Woolfenden** 39
DEFENDER

COUNTRY: England   DOB: 21/10/1998

Woolfenden signed his first professional contract for the 2017/18 season. He went on to make his first team debut in the 2-0 win over Luton Town in the Carabao Cup on 8th August 2017.

Chris **Smith** 40
DEFENDER

COUNTRY: England   DOB: 21/02/1998

Smith signed a professional deal for the 2017/18 season and joined the list of impressive youngsters who made their debuts against Crystal Palace at the beginning of the season.

Conor**McKendry**

41
MIDFIELDER

COUNTRY: Northern Ireland   DOB: 21/10/1998

The exciting winger or forward has represented Northern Ireland at Under-16 and Under-17 level. He recently signed a professional deal for the 2017/18 season.

Shane**McLoughlin**

42
FORWARD

COUNTRY: Republic of Ireland   DOB: 01/03/1997

Shane has represented the Republic of Ireland at Under-18 and Under-19 level. He made his first team debut at the start of the 2017/18 season.

George**Fowler**

43
DEFENDER

COUNTRY: England   DOB: 20/11/1997

Defender George progressed through the academy as a scholar. He made his debut against Crystal Palace in the Carabao Cup on 22nd August 2017. A loan move to Aldershot Town at the start of the 2017/18 season will offer valuable first team experience.

Emyr**Huws**

44
MIDFIELDER

COUNTRY: Wales   DOB: 30/09/1993

A box-to-box midfielder, Huws made his stay at Portman Road permanent in the summer of 2017, following a successful loan spell in the second half of the 16/17 campaign. He scored three times during his initial loan spell with the Club, including a Goal of the Season contender against Newcastle.

IPSWICH TOWN FOOTBALL CLUB

Arnold Muhren and Frans Thijssen are unquestionably the finest midfield pairing to pull on the famous blue and white shirt and represent Ipswich Town Football Club.

DOUBLE

For a three-season spell between 1979 and 1982 Dutch maestros Muhren and Thijssen produced a midfield masterclass at Portman Road that lives fondly in the memory of those supporters who were fortunate enough to be watching Town in that era.

Muhren was the first to arrive in Suffolk, after joining from FC Twente for a fee of £150,000 in 1978. Manager Bobby Robson swiftly got his team to adapt to the Dutchman's style of play and Town's performances were transformed. Muhren simply possessed a wand of a left-foot and developed an almost telepathic understanding with Alan Brazil, creating so many goals for the Scottish striker.

When Thijssen joined his colleague Muhren at Portman Road in 1979, the team was complete. The pair were the best midfield partnership in England, and contributed massively to the team's 1980/81 season, when they won the UEFA Cup and fell agonisingly short in both the First Division and the FA Cup.

1981 UEFA Cup Final, Second Leg.
AZ Alkmaar v Ipswich Town.
Thijssen is congratulated after scoring the first goal.

THIJSSEN

Muhren's almost inch-perfect passing and delivery from set piece situations was complemented by Thijssen's tight dribbling skills which saw him emerge with the ball from the most tricky of situations.

ACTS

In short, Muhren and Thijssen were the engine room of a Town side playing some of the most attractive and effective pass and move football ever witnessed.

The partnership came to an end in 1982 when Muhren was transferred to Manchester United. His four years at Portman Road saw him make a total of 214 appearances for Town, scoring 29 goals. Muhren went on to enjoy FA Cup glory with United in 1983 and his magical left foot was still in fine fettle in 1988, as he helped inspire Holland to European Championship glory.

After arriving from FC Twente a few months later then his compatriot, Thijssen then played a season without Muhren by his side before joining Nottingham Forest via a brief spell with Vancouver Whitecaps.

The 1980/81 UEFA Cup success was arguably Thijssen's greatest moment with Town as he netted goals in both legs of the final to secure that 5-4 aggregate triumph. Fittingly he was voted Footballer of the Year at the conclusion of that classic campaign. In total Thijssen played 170 games for the club scoring 16 goals.

Both players have been inducted into the club's Hall of Fame in recognition of their outstanding contribution to Ipswich Town.

Muhren and Thijssen hold the UEFA Cup trophy!

& MUHREN

2
DOMINIC
IORFA

**A TRUE PORTMAN ROAD LEGEND,
HERE ARE SIX FACTS BEHIND MICK MILLS'
ENDURING POPULARITY
AMONG TOWN FANS...**

1. RECORD APPEARANCE MAKER

Mick Mills began his marathon 741-game Ipswich Town career aged just 17 when he made his debut in a 5-2 Second Division victory over Wolves in 1966. Over a 16 year period he would go on to write his name in the record books as the club's top appearance maker. His 741 games for the club is a total unlikely to ever be surpassed.

2. PROMOTION WINNER

Having spent his late teens establishing himself in the first team at Portman Road, Mills achieved the first of his many successes with the club in 1968 as Town won promotion to the old First Division. The 1967/68 season saw Town crowned Second Division champions as they held off a strong challenge from QPR to take the title by just one point.

3. SETTING THE STANDARD

Following the arrival of Bobby Robson as manager, Mills soon struck up a close working relationship with his new boss and was named team captain in 1971. The 1972/73 campaign then saw Town finish fourth in the top flight and win the Texaco Cup as the seeds were sown for the most successful era in the club's history.

4. CUP WINNING CAPTAIN

On Saturday 6 May 1978 Mick Mills became the first, and to-date only, Ipswich Town captain to hold aloft the FA Cup. Town were underdogs when they faced Arsenal and their star England striker Malcolm Macdonald in the Wembley showpiece. However, a single goal from Roger Osborne and a stout defensive display saw Mills lead his men up the famous Wembley steps to collect the cup.

5. UEFA CUP GLORY

In the halcyon days under Bobby Robson when Town were consistent title challengers, the club came within touching distance of winning the First Division title as they ended the campaign as runners-up, four points behind champions Aston Villa. Despite that league title near-miss, Mills and his teammates railed to end the season on a positive note by winning the UEFA Cup. Over a two legged final against AZ Alkmaar, Town ran out 5-4 winners on aggregate and Mills was presented with the trophy on an unforgettable evening in Amsterdam.

6. FOR CLUB AND COUNTRY

As an accomplished defender for one of the country's top league sides and a born leader, it was of little surprise that Mills would go on to win international recognition with England. Mills was handed his international debut by Alf Ramsey and proceeded to win 42 caps for his country. He also captained the England team in the 1982 World Cup finals in Spain.

MICK MILLS'
SIX STEPS TO STARDOM

CHAMPIONSHIP KEY PLAYERS

ALEX SMITHIES
QPR

Now 27, former England U19 international Alex, was at one time rated as one of the country's hottest young goalkeepers after breaking into Huddersfield's first eleven when just 17. Despite a lot of interest, he stayed with the West Yorkshire side, playing 274 games for the Terriers until his 2015 move to the capital.

KEIREN WESTWOOD
SHEFFIELD WEDNESDAY

Keiren's excellent displays between the sticks have been rewarded with over 20 international caps for the Republic of Ireland. The excellent shot-stopper has made over 130 appearances each for Sheffield Wednesday, Coventry City and Carlisle United as well as being honoured with the Player of the Year award at each club!

ADAM DAVIES
BARNSLEY

Although Adam was born in Germany, the 25-year-old comes from a Welsh family and although he's yet to debut, he has been a part of several Wales squads. After starting his career at Everton followed by a spell with Sheffield Wednesday, Davies is now a real safe pair of hands for the Tykes with over 100 appearances behind him.

goalkeepers

The value of a great goalkeeper just can't be underestimated. We've selected six top stoppers who will look to shine over the coming months.

FELIX WIEDWALD
LEEDS UNITED

After making the move to Yorkshire from Werder Bremen in the summer, former Germany U20 international Felix really caught the eye and did so well that he was chosen ahead of Leeds United's ex-England 'keeper Rob Green. The imposing 6'3" goalie has also played in Germany with MSV Duisburg and Eintracht Frankfurt.

SCOTT CARSON
DERBY COUNTY

The former England goalkeeper is still one of the best 'keepers around. Scott commands his penalty area and has a real presence on the pitch. After starting out with a handful of appearances for both Leeds United and Liverpool, Carson has now played over 400 career games both in England and Turkey.

VITO MANNONE
READING

Vito came to England from Atalanta and continued his career at Arsenal. Following loan spells with Barnsley and Hull City, he went north to Sunderland where he was the hero of the Black Cats' run to the 2014 League Cup final, starring in their semi-final shoot-out win against Manchester United at Old Trafford. Player of the Year at the Stadium of Light that year, Mannone moved to the Madejski Stadium in the summer of 2017.

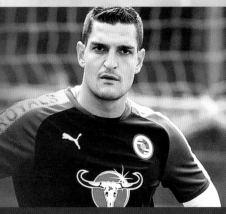

MICHAEL DAWSON
HULL CITY

Former England and Spurs centre-back, Michael made his name with Nottingham Forest before moving to the capital in 2005. The commanding defender has been voted Player of the Year with both Tottenham and the Tigers as well as winning the League Cup with Spurs a decade ago. The City skipper's consistant displays have seen him selected for the PFA Team of the Year at both ends of his career, in 2003 and 2016.

JOHN TERRY
ASTON VILLA

John is a modern-day legend. After over 700 appearances for Chelsea, and 78 for England, he had plenty of choices after leaving Stamford Bridge, but was convinced of Aston Villa's attractions by Steve Bruce, once a top-class centre-back himself. He has won everything going with Chelsea and has more individual awards than one trophy cabinet can hold.

RYAN SESSEGNON
FULHAM

Probably the best young player in the Championship, London-born Sessegnon is the cousin of the former Sunderland and WBA, Benin international Stephane Sessegnon. Ryan debuted for Fulham in August 2016 when he was only 16. Despite playing at left-back, he was joint top scorer at the 2017 European U19 tournament won with England.

defenders

Protecting a lead, battling for that all important clean sheet and trying to help support their attack-minded teammates - here are six top quality Championship defenders to look out for.

SOULEYMANE BAMBA
CARDIFF CITY

Experienced Ivory Coast international centre-back Souleymane was born in France and began his playing career with Paris Saint-Germain before a move to Dunfermline. After plying his trade in Scotland, England, Turkey and Italy, Bamba made Wales the sixth country he has called home when he signed for Neil Warnock's Bluebirds.

NATHAN BAKER
BRISTOL CITY

After 13 years and over 100 games for Aston Villa, former England U21 international left-footed centre-back Nathan Baker signed for the Robins last summer after spending the previous season on loan at Ashton Gate. Brave and committed, Villa's loss is certainly Bristol's gain.

JOHN EGAN
BRENTFORD

The Republic of Ireland international centre-back has the happy knack of chipping in with his share of goals. He is a proper centre-back, a leader with a real hunger to keep the ball out of the net. John's dad was a famous Gaelic footballer while his mother has a League of Ireland winners medal with Cork Rangers, so it's no surprise he is a talented lad destined for the top.

21

CHEIKH NDOYE
BIRMINGHAM CITY

A commanding 6ft 3ins powerhouse in the centre of midfield, Senegal international Cheikh moved to St Andrew's in 2017 from French club Angers who he skippered in last season's Coupe de France final, narrowly losing 1-0 to all-conquering Paris Saint-Germain. He previously played for Creteil with whom he won the Championnat National (the third division of the French football) in 2013.

AIDEN McGEADY
SUNDERLAND

With almost 100 caps for the Republic of Ireland, Aiden is one of the most magical wingers in the championship. In 2010 he commanded a fee of almost £10m when joining Spartak Moscow from Celtic with whom he had won seven trophies. He arrived at the Stadium of Light from Everton after playing for Black Cats boss Simon Grayson last season on loan to Preston.

DANIEL JOHNSON
PRESTON NORTH END

Originally from Kingston, Jamaica, Daniel is unmistakable with his very long hair and equally unmistakable with the energy he shows all over the pitch. He progressed through the Aston Villa academy and went on a trio of loans before Preston signed him in January 2015. Eight goals from midfield from 23 games that season helped power Preston to promotion.

midfielders

The Championship is packed with top-class midfield performers - we've chosen six midfield maestros who could well be real star turns for their respective clubs this season.

NATHAN THOMAS
SHEFFIELD UNITED

A talented and exciting winger, Nathan made the jump from, just relegated from League Two Hartlepool, to just promoted from League One Sheffield United and got off to a flying start with a debut goal in a League Cup win over Walsall. He likes to score the spectacular, finding the back of the net nine times for struggling Hartlepool last season and it's only a matter of time until Thomas is a fans' favourite at Bramall Lane.

RUBEN NEVES
WOLVES

Wanderers' Portuguese international record-signing midfielder from Porto cost a reported £15.8m in 2017. Neves is just 20, but reads the game like a seasoned professional and seems destined for the top. Wolves hope this natural leader will guide them to the Premier League. Ruben is also the youngest player to captain a team in the Champions League, Porto at the age of 18.

JEM KARACAN
BOLTON WANDERERS

Jem is at his best when he's hassling and disrupting the opposition's midfield with his typically high-energy performance. London-born to an English mother and Turkish father, Jem has played for Turkey at junior levels and been in full international squads, but has yet to make his full international debut. He has played club football in Turkey as well as Engla and after starting over 150 games for Reading he joined Bolton from Galatasary in 2017.

CHAMPIONSHIP KEY PLAYERS

MARVIN SORDELL
BURTON ALBION

Still only 26, Marvin seems to have been around for a long time. He represented Great Britain at the 2012 London Olympics and has also played for England at U21 level. He made his name with Watford and once commanded a big money move into the Premier League with Bolton. He is a consistent and versatile performer who likes to shoot from distance.

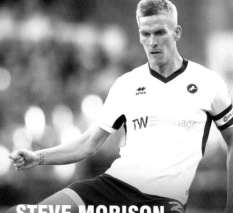

DARYL MURPHY
NOTTINGHAM FOREST

The Republic of Ireland international was the Championship's top scorer in 2014/15 with Ipswich Town when the targetman's power and pace also earned him the Tractor Boys' Player of the Year award. He won Premier League promotion with Newcastle United last season and Sunderland in 2007 and also had a spell with Celtic in the SPL at the start of the decade.

STEVE MORISON
MILLWALL

33-year-old Steve is a Lions legend. He is now in his third spell with the club and is the reigning Millwall Player of the Year. The towering striker has scored over 230 goals in a career that started in 2001 with Northampton Town and has seen him play for England at 'C' level (non-league), before becoming a full international with Wales.

forwards

Goals win games and when it comes to finding the back of the net at Championship level they don't come much sharper than these six great goal getters.

BRITT ASSOMBALONGA
MIDDLESBROUGH

Britt is arguably, considered the best striker outside the Premier League. He is a proven goalscorer in the Championship, scoring 30 goals in 47 league starts for Forest. The Teessiders invested £15m to bring in the son of a former Zaire international and if he stays injury-free, could fire Boro back into the Premier League.

NELSON OLIVEIRA
NORWICH CITY

The Portugal international is a threatening striker, quick off the mark with first-class technique and neat footwork. Nelson, who started with Benfica, had six loans with clubs in Portugal, France, England and Wales, before committing his future to the Carrow Road club in 2016. He scored 15 times in 31 games in his first season as a Canary and commenced the current campaign with three goals in his first three matches.

MARTYN WAGHORN
IPSWICH TOWN

The former England U21 international returned to the English league last summer after two years in Scotland with Rangers where he won a Player of the Year award to go with the Young Player of the Year trophy he won with Leicester. Martyn has the ability to play anywhere across the front four and his good scoring record continued this season with four goals in his first three Championship games.

GOAL OF THE SEASON

Tom Lawrence

QPR vs Ipswich · 2nd January 2017

Travelling fans witnessed an absolute stunner in what was Town's first game of 2017.

The Blues were 1-0 down after Idrissa Sylla had volleyed the home side in front in the 30th minute. Step forward Tom Lawrence to spectacularly equalise early in the second-half.

Picking up a pass from Cole Skuse and with his back to the goal, Lawrence turned and drove forward before unleashing a pile driver from 25 yards out. The ball arrowed across the goal toward the top corner, flew past keeper Alex Smithies, and cracked the inside of the post before rippling the back of the net.

Although QPR would eventually go on to score a late winner Town fans could take solace in the fact that they had been there to witness a truly sensational goal.

This was confirmed at Town's end of season awards ceremony. The Leicester loanee swept up in the goal of the season category, his strike against QPR picking up the gong and his goals against Blackburn and Preston coming tied for second place. His knack for the spectacular also earned him the Players' Player of the Year award to round off a hugely successful loan spell with the Blues.

IPSWICH TOWN
FOOTBALL CLUB

DAVID
McGOLDRICK
10

Can you identify...

26

..all of these
Ipswich Town stars?

WHO ARE YER

TRAINING TO WIN

Footballers are finely-tuned athletes with impressive skills which they need to demonstrate under pressure. They have to be physically and mentally strong.

The world's top sports-stars face tough challenges in their chosen field, but they can be very different to those that a footballer has to face. In sports such as golf, athletics and even tennis or a team game like cricket, you have no-one physically trying to stop you when you're attempting to play the game.

However, think about what you have to do as a footballer. You have to have the ability to control the ball, even when it comes to you at speed or a difficult angle. You have to be able to pass over short and long distances. You have to be able to head the ball. Not every player can do it all, but at least some members of the team have to be able to shoot well and tackle too.

All this would be hard enough without having your opponent doing his utmost to stop you - holding you, pushing you, knocking you off balance and quite possibly fouling you. So a footballer has to have strength and speed as well as skill.

To become a professional footballer, firstly, you have to have bundles of skill which you've probably spent all your life developing, but you also have to be extremely fit. Footballers do all kinds of exercise to get fit, and stay fit. They work in the gym to build up their strength and they also work with fitness coaches who keep them in peak physical condition.

They have to be very careful to follow a healthy diet. If they don't, it makes it hard for them to stay match fit. They avoid foods with lots of fat, so they rarely eat things like crisps, chocolate, chips and burgers, if at all.

Once they have reached full fitness for the start of the season, footballers usually train for about two hours a day, four or five days a week if they have one game a week. It is important that they also rest at the right times or they won't feel at their best during games. Some players will also do other exercises like pilates or yoga to help them stay supple.

There is a lot to being a professional footballer. Staying in peak condition requires a lot of dedication and players who look after themselves well by eating healthily and training hard will be able to give their team 100% on the pitch.

JOE **14**
GARNER

FOOTBALL 50

IPSWICH TOWN
FOOTBALL CLUB

```
S U B S T I T U T E I S R E D L E I F D I M
M A A Z P L E A O S U J Y O Y T N D T R K O
A Q E X T R A T I M E R L C K J A U D I M E
N B L C A C A D E M Y K F Y U K O B C B N P
O N I E S A J W R T P E X R T G D K H B P B
F R F J A P H I A E M R Y C U C O C A L T L
T H I W Y T D B K W S T O D Y F B R L I E I
H D N E P A R X J B I S C M F A U O L N E T
E D A Z L I N E S M A N I T O F D G E G H R
M B L D S N W A E C Q I U N A T P U N Q S A
A I W Y H C O R N E R F L A G O I M G Z N N
T E H E A D E R V L H Y S R I R C O E R A S
C B I M J E E L U R E D I S F F O K N V E F
H G S G Q F P R N U A L K L G I H O B M L E
F R T U F E L N B T F E R E G A N A M A C R
M E L K E N G F B Y D H T D A F V G O H J W
Y K E F C D R P O C M F H L H J W G A B H I
S I O W O E K S P U I A O A V S N F D M I N
A R W M N R Q N R P L H T U O E M S R T J D
O T K C I K E E R F Y T D C D J Y B A G T O
G S O V T C A D T B R X N L H S F A C U P W
K A M P Q E T I C I E F O M R N G E W B S U
C I A M S K M R C A S G C G O U K O O C E M
I Y E J A E R K D I R F H S R E Y A L P V C
K C T E P D R G B F K D A E U G A E L E R S
R E T L T N W T J N G E Q U A L I S E R E H
O Y S P A I A W N G S R C V S F G L Y F S R
S S R N T N H L H E L S U N U T M E G U E N
S K I J S J E V R L C W A S P O L S O F R J
I K F P F H M P L K U F E H E L A O E T I M
C R O S S B A R S C T T M R O J I R W T Q N
S O I R M E X I C A N W A V E P E O L D K P
G A S U N N A E R T U B R E P E E K L A O G
```

Word list:

Academy
Captain
Centre Spot
Challenge
Clean Sheet
Corner Flag
Crossbar
Defender
Derby Match
Dressing Room
Dribbling
Dugout
Equaliser
Extra Time
FA Cup
Fans
Final Whistle
First Team
Fixture
Foul
Free Kick
Goalkeeper
Golden Goal
Half Time
Hat-trick
Header
Injury Time
Kick-off
League
Linesman
Manager
Man of the Match
Mexican Wave
Midfielder
Nutmeg
Offside Rule
Penalty
Players
Pre-season
Promotion
Red Card
Referee
Reserves
Scissor Kick
Striker
Substitute
Tackle
Transfer Window
Volley
Yellow Card

IPSWICH TOWN

THE TEAM

Back Row (left to right): Dick Parker (Academy Operations), Tom Adeyemi, Tommy Smith, Dominic Iorfa, Bartosz Bialkowski, Michael Crowe, Dean Gerken, Adam Webster, Jordan Spence, Emyr Huws, James Pullen (Kitman),

Middle Row (left to right): Ken Goody (U23's Kitman), Matt Byard (Head Physio), Malcolm Webster (GK Coach), Luke Hyam, Kevin Bru, Joe Garner, David McGoldrick, Luke Chambers, Cole Skuse, Myles Kenlock, Jonas Knudsen, Flynn Downes, Gerard Nash (U23's Manager), Alex Chapman (Assistant Physio), Lee Catling (First team Massage Therapist).

Front Row (left to right): Will Stephenson (Head Analyst), Tristan Nydam, Freddie Sears, Andre Dozzell, Dave Bowman (Director of Football), Mick McCarthy (Manager), Terry Connor (Assistant Manager), Danny Rowe, Grant Ward, Teddy Bishop, Andy Liddell (Fitness Coach).

PLAYER OF THE SEASON

Bartosz Bialkowski

Town keeper Bartosz Bialkowski was named the 'Supporters' Club Player of the Year' for the second season running. The keeper finished top of the poll, beating Leicester loanee Tom Lawrence who claimed second place.

Throughout the season 'Bart' added to his ever-growing collection of wonder saves with some inspirational displays and breathtaking stops. He played a key role in Town safely securing another season of Championship football.

In winning the award two years in a row he joins an exclusive list of players achieving that feat, featuring club legends John Wark, Kevin Beattie and Terry Butcher.

'Bart' showed how much the award meant to him personally by 'tweeting' out to fans shortly after the award ceremony. Town's Polish custodian said "I can't explain how I'm feeling atm! To win Player of the Year 2nd time in a row is something very special! Would like to thank everyone".

Bialkowski also picked up the 'Junior Blues Player of the Year' award. He has also agreed to be Junior Blues captain for the 2017/18 season, a role which will see him be the face of the Club's membership for youngsters.

Since the first Player of the Season award in 1973, the Ipswich Town faithful have witnessed many great footballing heroes grace the hallowed turf of Portman Road. Take a look at all the winners starting with Blues legend Kevin Beattie...

1972/73	Kevin Beattie
1973/74	Kevin Beattie
1974/75	Colin Viljoen
1975/76	Allan Hunter
1976/77	George Burley
1977/78	Mick Mills
1978/79	Arnold Mühren
1979/80	Frans Thijssen
1980/81	Paul Cooper
1981/82	Alan Brazil
1982/83	Paul Mariner
1983/84	Trevor Putney
1984/85	Terry Butcher
1985/86	Terry Butcher
1986/87	Romeo Zondervan
1987/88	Frank Yallop
1988/89	John Wark
1989/90	John Wark
1990/91	David Linighan
1991/92	John Wark
1992/93	Mick Stockwell
1993/94	John Wark
1994/95	Craig Forrest
1995/96	Simon Milton
1996/97	Mauricio Taricco
1997/98	Matt Holland
1998/99	Jamie Clapham
1999/00	James Scowcroft
2000/01	Marcus Stewart
2001/02	Mark Venus
2002/03	Matt Holland
2003/04	Ian Westlake
2004/05	Shefki Kuqi
2005/06	Fabian Wilnis
2006/07	Sylvain Legwinski
2007/08	Jonathan Walters
2008/09	Richard Wright
2009/10	Gareth McAuley
2010/11	Jimmy Bullard
2011/12	Aaron Cresswell
2012/13	Tommy Smith
2013/14	Christophe Berra
2014/15	Daryl Murphy
2015/16	Bartosz Bialkowski
2016/17	Bartosz Bialkowski

CURRENT TOWN SKIPPER LUKE CHAMBERS IS A FANS' FAVOURITE, HERE ARE SIX FACTORS BEHIND THE CAPTAIN'S ONGOING POPULARITY...

1. CHOOSING TOWN

Chambers was very much a man in demand when his contract at Nottingham Forest expired in the summer of 2012. The much-admired defender was approached by a number of other Championship clubs but after meeting then Ipswich manager Paul Jewell, he was convinced his future was best served at Portman Road. He passed a medical and agreed a three-year contract in July 2012.

2. SKIPPER ON THE SCORESHEET

It didn't take long for Chambers to make a positive impact at Portman Road. When injury ruled skipper Carlos Edwards out of Town's home match with Huddersfield Town in September 2012, Chambers was handed the captain's armband for the first time and marked the occasion by scoring his first goal for the club in a 2-2 draw with the Terriers.

3. MR CONSISTENT

Despite a change of manager in a difficult season for the club, Chambers soon established himself as a mainstay of the Town back four during his debut season with the club. Under the guidance of new manager Mick McCarthy, Town fought off the threat or relegation and secured a mid-table finish with Chambers part of a defensive unit that kept 12 clean sheets in the final 22 games of the season.

4. CLUB CAPTAIN

After two seasons with the Blues, Chambers was named club captain at the start of the 2014/15 campaign following the departure of Carlos Edwards. With Chambers being an experienced pro and popular character in the dressing room coupled with his respect from the club's supporters, this was not a difficult choice for manager McCarthy.

5. TOP SIX FINISH

Chambers enjoyed a memorable first full season as Town skipper with the team exceeding expectations and securing a place in the end-of-season play-offs. An East Anglian derby meeting with rivals Norwich City stood between Town and Wembley but sadly it was the Canaries who came out on top. Despite that disappointment, Chambers helped rally the Town troops again in 2015/16 as once again they pushed for a play-off place but ended the season agonisingly close in seventh.

6. CARRY ON CHAMBO!

During his five years at Portman Road, Chambers has become a cult hero with supporters who particularly enjoy his trademark fist pump celebrations that greet Town victories. In May 2017 he agreed a new two-year contract with the Club and declared his desire to see Town competing for a Play-Off place again in 2017/18.

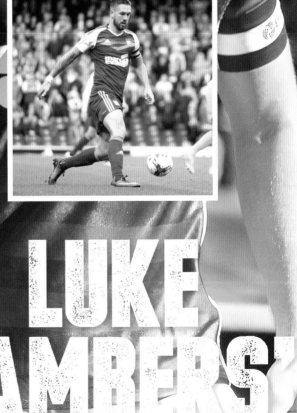

LUKE CHAMBERS'

SIX STEPS TO STARDOM

GRANT**18**
WARD

CHAMPIONSHIP

ASTON VILLA

Which England and Chelsea legend did Aston Villa sign at the start of this season?

1 ANSWER

Aston Villa won the European Cup in 1981. Did they beat Bayern Munich, Barcelona or Real Madrid in the final?

2 ANSWER

Who is the former Sunderland manager who started the season as Villa manager?

3 ANSWER

BARNSLEY

During the summer Barnsley signed Ezekiel Fryers from which Premier League London club?

5 ANSWER

Who is Barnsley's captain?

4 ANSWER

Who is the Tykes' manager?

6 ANSWER

BIRMINGHAM CITY

When did Birmingham City last win the League Cup?

8 ANSWER

Who scored Blues first league goal this season?

7 ANSWER

City completed a record signing on transfer deadline day, summer 2017, who was it?

9 ANSWER

BOLTON WANDERERS

How many times have Bolton won the FA Cup?

10 ANSWER

Bolton reached the League Cup final in 2004 but lost to which club who are also now in the Championship?

11 ANSWER

Name the manager who led Bolton to promotion in 2017 in his first season at the club.

12 ANSWER

BRENTFORD

Brentford are West London rivals of QPR who they knocked out of this season's Carabao Cup away from home. Did they win 3-1, 4-1 or 5-1?

13 ANSWER

Who is Brentford's Number 9 striker this season?

14 ANSWER

Who was the manager of Brentford from 2013 to 2015 who went on to manage Rangers and Nottingham Forest?

15 ANSWER

BRISTOL CITY

Which Premier League team did City knock out of the Carabao Cup away from home in the second round this season?

17 ANSWER

Who was Bristol City's Player of the Season in 2016/17?

16 ANSWER

Who scored 23 times for Bristol City last season on loan from Chelsea?

18 ANSWER

CHALLENGE

Let's see how well you know the Tractor Boys and their Championship rivals...

BURTON ALBION

Who was Burton's first summer signing ahead of the 2017/18 season?

20 ANSWER

Which former England international began the season as Burton's manager?

19 ANSWER

Which former Liverpool and Villa player signed for Burton at the start of the season?

21 ANSWER

CARDIFF CITY

Cardiff City are the Bluebirds but what colour were their shirts between 2012 and 2015?

22 ANSWER

Who was the manager who inspired Cardiff to maximum points from their first four league games of this season?

23 ANSWER

Who was the Chile international midfielder who moved from Cardiff to Inter Milan in 2014 and stayed with the Italian giants until 2017?

24 ANSWER

DERBY COUNTY

Which Derby player scored the opening goal at the Stadium of Light this season?

25 ANSWER

In what year did Derby win the FA Cup?

26 ANSWER

Who is the former England international Derby re-signed for a second spell at the club at the start of this season?

27 ANSWER

FULHAM

Who is Fulham's No 1 this season?

29 ANSWER

Which Spanish side beat Fulham in the final of the 2010 Europa League?

28 ANSWER

Who is Fulham's No 10 and their captain this season?

30 ANSWER

HULL CITY

Which country did Leonid Slutsky manage before taking over at Hull?

32 ANSWER

Hull reached the FA Cup final in 2014 but lost to which London club?

33 ANSWER

What is Hull's nickname?

31 ANSWER

IPSWICH TOWN

Who scored Town's first league goal this season?

34 ANSWER

Ipswich went from the third division to top flight champions in six years under the manager who later won the World Cup for England. Who was that?

35 ANSWER

In which season did the Tractor Boys win the FA Cup?

36 ANSWER

LEEDS UNITED

What is Leeds United's club anthem?

37 ANSWER

Who is captaining the Whites this season?

Between 1965 and 1974 how many times did Leeds finish in the top two of the league?

38 ANSWER

39 ANSWER

MIDDLESBROUGH

Which Spanish team beat Middlesbrough in the 2006 Europa League final?

41 ANSWER

Who did Boro sign on a season-long loan from Swansea City in July 2017?

40 ANSWER

Which major trophy did Boro win in 2004?

42 ANSWER

MILLWALL

Who did Millwall play in the 2004 FA Cup final?

44 ANSWER

Millwall began this season with one of their former Players of the Year as manager. Who?

43 ANSWER

What is Millwall's nickname?

45 ANSWER

NORWICH CITY

Which team did Head Coach, Daniel Farke, manage before joining City this season?

46 ANSWER

How many League Cup finals have Norwich played in, two, three or four?

47 ANSWER

Who is the Canaries No 1 this season?

48 ANSWER

NOTTINGHAM FOREST

Which Premier League club did Forest defeat away from home in the Carabao Cup in August 2017?

49 ANSWER

Forest have twice won the European Cup (now the Champions League). True or false?

50 ANSWER

Who is the former Brighton, Leeds and Sunderland midfielder Forest signed in August 2017?

51 ANSWER

PRESTON NORTH END

Who was the future Everton and Manchester United manager who won the Division Two title with Preston in 2000?

53 ANSWER

Who was Preston's top scorer last season?

52 ANSWER

Preston did it first in 1996, Wolves equalled it in 1988 and Burnley, Sheffield United and Portsmouth have done it since. What is the feat these five clubs have achieved?

54 ANSWER

CHALLENGE

Let's see how well you know the Tractor Boys and their Championship rivals...

QUEENS PARK RANGERS

Which defender did Rangers pay a club record £12.5m for in 2013 only to sell him later that year?

56 ANSWER

Who is QPR's captain this season?

55 ANSWER

Which of the following managers have not managed QPR: Harry Redknapp, Mark Hughes, Martin O'Neill and Ian Holloway?

57 ANSWER

READING

Which former Manchester United defender was manager of Reading at the start of the season?

58 ANSWER

What position in the Championship did Reading finish in last season?

59 ANSWER

Who did Reading sign from Sunderland during the summer?

60 ANSWER

SHEFFIELD UNITED

Who is the Blades' No 9 striker this season?

61 ANSWER

How many points did Sheffield United earn in winning League One last season: 95, 100 or 105?

62 ANSWER

Goalkeeper Jamal Blackman is on a season long loan to Sheffield United from which Premier League London club?

63 ANSWER

SHEFFIELD WEDNESDAY

Sheffield Wednesday are one of the oldest clubs in the world. In 2017 they celebrated a major anniversary. How many years old were the club in 2017?

65 ANSWER

Who was Sheffield Wednesday's first 2017 summer signing?

64 ANSWER

Adding together Sheffield Wednesday's top flight league titles, FA Cup and League Cup wins, how many major trophies have they won: 6, 7 or 8?

66 ANSWER

SUNDERLAND

How many other current Championship clubs have Sunderland met in FA Cup finals?

68 ANSWER

Who did Sunderland sign from West Brom on August 2017 transfer deadline day ?

67 ANSWER

Which two academy produced players scored their first goals for the club in August 2017?

69 ANSWER

WOLVERHAMPTON WANDERERS

Who were last season's League Cup finalists who Wolves knocked out of this season's Carabao Cup in August?

70 ANSWER

Between 1950 and 1960 how many times did Wolves finish in the top two of the top flight?

71 ANSWER

Who is the Portuguese midfielder Wolves paid almost £16m in the summer of 2017?

72 ANSWER

FREDDIE
20 SEARS

SUCCESS WITH TOWN AS A PLAYER AND MANAGER, HERE ARE SIX FACTORS BEHIND THE MAKING OF AN IPSWICH LEGEND...

1. TACKLING THE BEST

George Burley was never one to shirk a challenge and he proved that from the moment he first pulled on an Ipswich shirt. Tasked with marking the legendary George Best on his Town debut against Manchester United at Old Trafford might have seen many a young defender wilt but not Burley who gave an impressive performance and would go on to amass 500 games for Town.

2. CUP WINNER

Burley etched his name into Ipswich Town folklore by helping Bobby Robson's team overcome the odds to defeat Arsenal in the 1978 FA Cup final. Burley and his fellow defenders produced an excellent defensive display to provide the platform for Roger Osborne's 77th minute goal to hand Town FA Cup glory.

3. EURO HERO

Burley was a mainstay of the Town defence during the incredible 1980/81 campaign as Ipswich went in search of both domestic and European glory. Town fell short in their bid for the First Division title and exited at the semi-final stage of the FA Cup. However, they landed the UEFA Cup following an exciting run to the final where they eventually defeated AZ Alkmaar over two legs. Injury ruled Burley out of the final but his contribution to the UEFA Cup run and the season over all always sees him referred to as one of Town's Euro heroes.

4. FOURTH TIME LUCKY

After a successful playing career came to an end, Burley cut his teeth in management with Ayr United and Colchester United before returning to Portman Road as manager in 1994. He led the club to three play-off semi-finals before eventually guiding the team to Premier League promotion at the fourth attempt with a Wembley triumph over Barnsley in 2000.

5. MANAGER OF THE YEAR

Under the management of Burley, Town enjoyed an excellent first season back in the Premier League in 2000/01. Despite being many pundits tip for relegation, Ipswich recorded a fifth place finish that saw them qualify for the UEFA Cup the following season. The team's achievements in 2000/01 saw Burley land the highly-coveted Manager of the Season award.

6. BACK IN EUROPE

The 2001/02 season saw Burley guide Town back into competitive European action as they completed in the UEFA Cup once again - the trophy the club famously won back in 1980/81. A memorable run saw Town defeat Torpedo Moscow and Helsingborg in the first and second rounds respectively before bowing out to Italian giants Inter Milan in the San Siro stadium.

GEORGE BURLEY'S
SIX STEPS TO STARDOM

WORLD CUP

WHEN THE SEASON COMES TO AN END IN MAY, THE FOOTBALL DOESN'T STOP!

When Ipswich Town's campaign is over and the Championship prizes are handed out, you can sit back and get ready to watch the World's international super-stars take to the pitch for the 2018 FIFA World Cup which starts on 14 June.

Just to get you in the mood, try this World Cup quiz!

1930

The first World Cup was won by the host nation Uruguay, but who did they defeat 4-2 in the Final?

1950

During England's first-ever World Cup in Brazil, they were beaten 1-0 by a team of part-timers from which Country?

1966

Ipswich Town's mascot is Bluey, but what was the name of the official World Cup mascot when England beat Germany 4-2 to win the World Cup?

1934

The host nation were victorious again! Italy beat Czechoslovakia 2-1, but do you know how many times the Italians have won the World Cup?

Which country scored 27 goals, the most of the tournament? Ferenc Puskás netted four of them!

1954

1970

Arguably the greatest World Cup final of all time was in 1970, when brilliant Brazil won 4-1. Who did they beat?

1938

Italy retained the trophy with a 4-2 victory over Hungary, in which European capital?

1958 & 1962

The same name went on the trophy in 1958 and 1962, the first and second of their record five wins. Who are they?

1974

The Dutch captain produced one of the World Cup's most iconic moments - a 180 degree wrong-footing turn that totally outwitted the defender. What is the move called?

QUIZ...

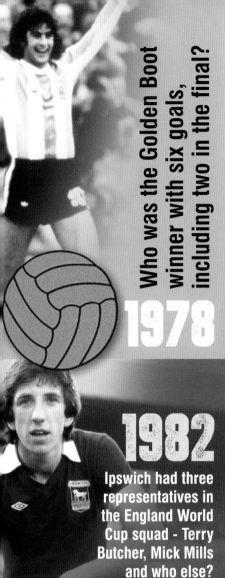

1978
Who was the Golden Boot winner with six goals, including two in the final?

1994
The record for most goals in a single match by one player is five, scored by Oleg Salenko as Cameroon were crushed 6-1 by which nation?

2006
One match, nicknamed 'the Battle of Nuremberg' ended nine-a-side as 16 yellow and four red cards were handed out. Who were the teams and what was the result?

1982
Ipswich had three representatives in the England World Cup squad - Terry Butcher, Mick Mills and who else?

1998
Who won the Golden Ball award for the tournament's best player?

2010
Only one country remained unbeaten throughout the whole tournament. Which Nation was it?

1986
Which legendary Argentinian scored twice to knock England out at the quarter-final stage 2-1?

2002
Which nation did former Tractor Boy Matt Holland represent in South Korea and Japan?

2014
Which country staged the last World Cup in 2014 and who are the World Cup holders?

1990
In the opening match, the holders Argentina suffered a shock 1-0 defeat by which African nation?

2018
Where are the World Cup finals going to be held next summer?

Town's centre back pairing of Terry Butcher and Russell Osman remain one of the finest defensive combinations in the club's history.

DOUBLE

The two players made a combined total of 736 appearances for the club with their finest hour being the 1980/81 UEFA Cup Final triumph over AZ Alkmaar.

Both players were born in 1958 and progressed through the youth and reserve team ranks at Portman Road to become key players in a highly successful era for Town.

With Butcher and Osman at the heart of the defence, the team consistently competed for the First Division title and also reached the semi-final of the FA Cup in the same season as they tasted European glory.

The two defenders also won full England caps while with Town and the most famous photo of Butcher is him with his white England shirt drenched in blood following a match with Sweden. A brave and fully committed defender - he also shed blood for Town at least a couple of times, during a career with Ipswich which ended with him in tears as the team was relegated in 1986. Butcher was a player who really cared and certainly had the club in his heart. Undoubtedly one of the first names on any supporters' greatest ever Town XI, Butcher was inducted to the club's Hall of Fame in 2010.

BUTCHER

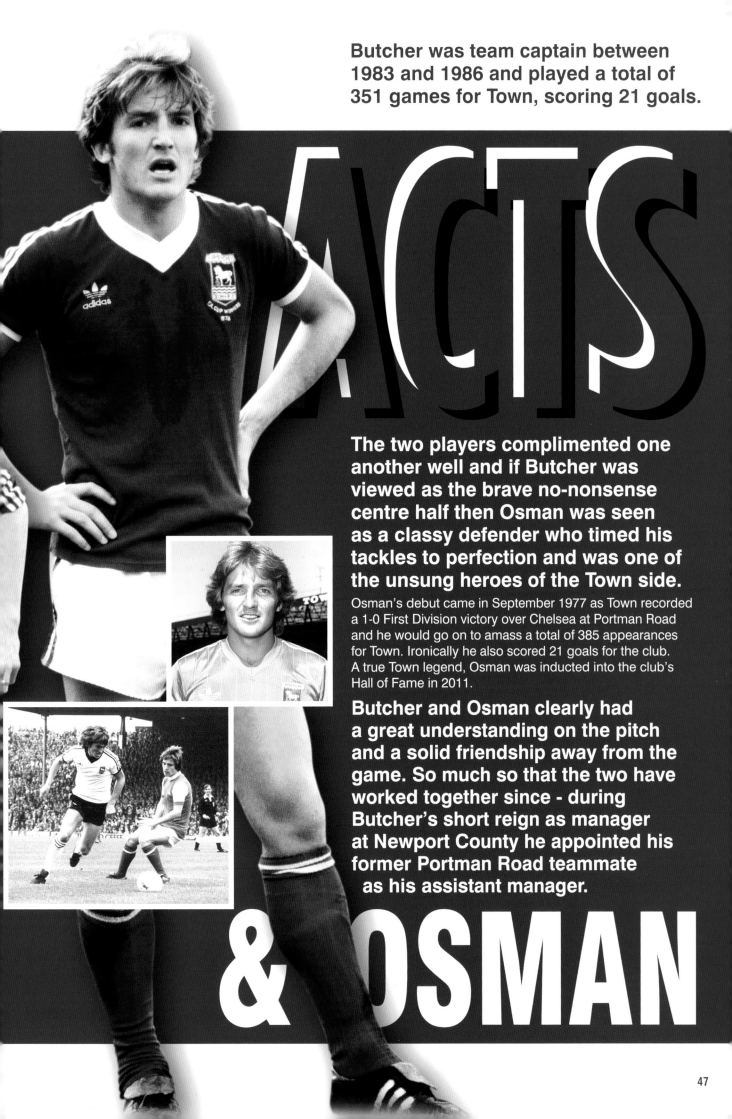

Butcher was team captain between 1983 and 1986 and played a total of 351 games for Town, scoring 21 goals.

FACTS

The two players complimented one another well and if Butcher was viewed as the brave no-nonsense centre half then Osman was seen as a classy defender who timed his tackles to perfection and was one of the unsung heroes of the Town side.

Osman's debut came in September 1977 as Town recorded a 1-0 First Division victory over Chelsea at Portman Road and he would go on to amass a total of 385 appearances for Town. Ironically he also scored 21 goals for the club. A true Town legend, Osman was inducted into the club's Hall of Fame in 2011.

Butcher and Osman clearly had a great understanding on the pitch and a solid friendship away from the game. So much so that the two have worked together since - during Butcher's short reign as manager at Newport County he appointed his former Portman Road teammate as his assistant manager.

& OSMAN

Design their kit,
add hair, be creative!

MAKE YOUR OWN
FOOZBALL
TEAM

IPSWICH TOWN
FOOTBALL CLUB

COLE **8**
SKUSE

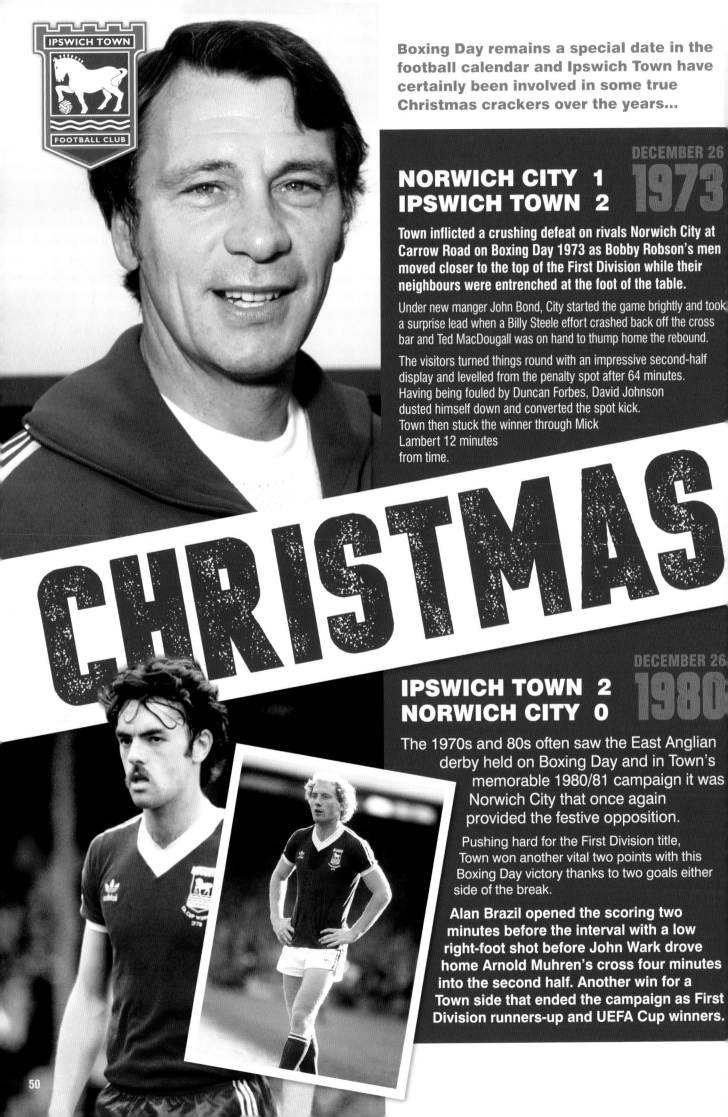

Boxing Day remains a special date in the football calendar and Ipswich Town have certainly been involved in some true Christmas crackers over the years...

DECEMBER 26 1973

NORWICH CITY 1
IPSWICH TOWN 2

Town inflicted a crushing defeat on rivals Norwich City at Carrow Road on Boxing Day 1973 as Bobby Robson's men moved closer to the top of the First Division while their neighbours were entrenched at the foot of the table.

Under new manger John Bond, City started the game brightly and took a surprise lead when a Billy Steele effort crashed back off the cross bar and Ted MacDougall was on hand to thump home the rebound.

The visitors turned things round with an impressive second-half display and levelled from the penalty spot after 64 minutes. Having being fouled by Duncan Forbes, David Johnson dusted himself down and converted the spot kick. Town then stuck the winner through Mick Lambert 12 minutes from time.

CHRISTMAS

DECEMBER 26 1980

IPSWICH TOWN 2
NORWICH CITY 0

The 1970s and 80s often saw the East Anglian derby held on Boxing Day and in Town's memorable 1980/81 campaign it was Norwich City that once again provided the festive opposition.

Pushing hard for the First Division title, Town won another vital two points with this Boxing Day victory thanks to two goals either side of the break.

Alan Brazil opened the scoring two minutes before the interval with a low right-foot shot before John Wark drove home Arnold Muhren's cross four minutes into the second half. Another win for a Town side that ended the campaign as First Division runners-up and UEFA Cup winners.

DECEMBER 26 1991

IPSWICH TOWN 2
CHARLTON ATHLETIC 0

Under the management of John Lyall, Ipswich picked up maximum points over the Christmas period during the club's 1991/92 Second Division title-winning season.

Leading goalscorer Chris Kiwomya was once again the toast of Portman Road as he netted both goals to seal this Boxing Day triumph over Charlton Athletic in front of a crowd of 13,826.

A 2-1 win at home to promotion-rivals Blackburn Rovers on December 28 was followed up by a 2-1 win at Port Vale on New Year's Day, thanks to another Kiwomya brace - it all made for a great festive spell and a wonderful season at Portman Road.

CRACKERS

DECEMBER 26 2001

IPSWICH TOWN 2
LEICESTER CITY 0

Town recorded a much needed home victory over Leicester City on Boxing Day 2001 as George Burley's team fought hard to maintain their Premier League status.

Ipswich went into the festive period on the back of five straight defeats but recorded a great 2-1 win away to Spurs on December 22 to lift spirits ahead of this must-win match with relegation rivals Leicester on Boxing Day.

Two goals early in the second-half from Marcus Bent on 48 minutes and Sixto Peralta seven minutes later secured a welcome three points. Town followed up this result with a 5-0 drubbing of Sunderland at Portman Road three days later to make it nine points from nine at the end of December. Festive cheer but no happy ending as Town suffered relegation at the end of the 2001/02 campaign.

WHAT'S GOING TO HAPPEN IN 2018?

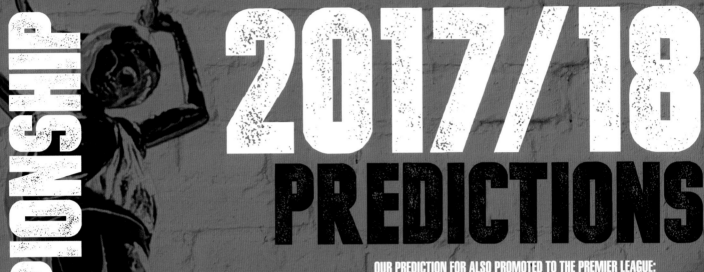

2017/18 PREDICTIONS

CHAMPIONSHIP

OUR PREDICTION FOR CHAMPIONSHIP WINNERS:

IPSWICH TOWN

YOUR PREDICTION:

OUR PREDICTION FOR ALSO PROMOTED TO THE PREMIER LEAGUE:

MIDDLESBROUGH & DERBY COUNTY

YOUR PREDICTION:

OUR PREDICTION FOR FA CUP WINNERS:

LIVERPOOL

YOUR PREDICTION:

FA CUP

PREMIER LEAGUE

OUR PREDICTION FOR PREMIER LEAGUE CHAMPIONS:

MANCHESTER UNITED

YOUR PREDICTION:

OUR PREDICTION FOR PREMIER LEAGUE RUNNERS-UP:

ARSENAL

YOUR PREDICTION:

OUR PREDICTION FOR PREMIER LEAGUE BOTTOM THREE:

WBA, STOKE CITY NEWCASTLE UNITED

YOUR PREDICTION:

OUR PREDICTION FOR LEAGUE CUP WINNERS:

CHELSEA

YOUR PREDICTION:

LEAGUE CUP

IPSWICH TOWN
FOOTBALL CLUB

9 MARTYN WAGHORN

Talented midfielder Kieron Dyer began his career with Ipswich Town and went on to enjoy Premier League fame and international honours with England.

Born in Ipswich on 29 December 1978, Dyer began his career at Portman Road and swiftly progressed through the youth and reserve teams to establish himself in Town's first team. His debut came on Boxing Day 1996, just three days before his 18th birthday as Town defeated Crystal Palace 3-1.

Once given a taste of first team football by boss George Burley, Dyer quickly established himself one of the top young players in the country. His development soon caught the eye of many Premier League scouts who often flocked to Portman Road to keep tabs on his growing reputation.

His undoubted ability was rewarded with international honours with England at under-21 level but Town's inability to win promotion to the Premier League ultimately left Dyer frustrated at not being able to showcase his talents at the highest level. After the club had suffered a hat-trick of play-off semi-final defeats, the local lad decided his future lay elsewhere and he completed a dream move to the Premier League in the summer of 1999 when he joined Newcastle United. Town received a then club record fee of £6m for his services.

Regular Premier League football at Newcastle coincided with Dyer winning his first full England cap on 4 September 1999 when he started in England's 6-0 win against Luxembourg. He was deployed out of position at right-back and was replaced at half time after injuring himself while setting up Alan Shearer's third goal of the game. The injury was not serious and he was able to make his second England appearance four days later, coming on as a late substitute in a 0-0 draw with Poland. Dyer went on to win a total of 33 caps for his country.

Dyer played over 200 games for Newcastle during an eight-year spell at St James' Park that was often interrupted by injuries. In August 2007 he secured a move to West Ham United but again a series of injury problems wrecked Dyer's time with the Hammers. He made a romantic return to Portman Road on loan in March 2011 in pursuit of both first team football and fitness but played just a further four games for the club. Brief spells at Queens Park Rangers and Middlesbrough followed before Dyer retired from the game.

Over his two spells at Portman Road, Dyer played a total of 117 games for the club scoring 12 goals.

MADE IN IPSWICH

IPSWICH TOWN FOOTBALL CLUB

You'd definitely recognise Portman Road but can you figure out which football club these grounds belong to...

HOME TURF

1

Team: _____
Ground: _____
Capacity: _____

2

Team: _____
Ground: _____
Capacity: _____

3

Team: _____
Ground: _____
Capacity: _____

4

Team: _____
Ground: _____
Capacity: _____

5

Team: _____
Ground: _____
Capacity: _____

6

Team: _____
Ground: _____
Capacity: _____

Team: _____
Ground: _____
Capacity: _____

Team: _____
Ground: _____
Capacity: _____

7

8

Team: _____
Ground: _____
Capacity: _____

9

Team: _____
Ground: _____
Capacity: _____

10

Team: _____
Ground: _____
Capacity: _____

ANSWERS ON PAGE 62

11

12

...as well as
their official name
and capacity?!

13

14

Team:

Ground:

Capacity:

Team:

Ground:

Capacity:

Team:

Ground:

Capacity:

Team:

Ground:

Capacity:

15

16

Team:

Ground:

Capacity:

Team:

Ground:

Capacity:

17

18

19

Team:

Ground:

Capacity:

Team:

Ground:

Capacity:

20

Team:

Ground:

Capacity:

Team:

Ground:

Capacity:

IPSWICH TOWN FOOTBALL CLUB

Five games to watch out for...

NORWICH CITY · AWAY
SUNDAY 18TH FEBRUARY

The East Anglian Derby. The first two match dates that fans look for when new season fixtures are announced - Norwich home and away. Town make the short trip to Carrow Road early in the new year and will be looking for victory over their arch rivals.

LEEDS UNITED · HOME
SATURDAY 13TH JANUARY

The Blues face Leeds United in their first home league game of 2018. With a big away following expected the home fans will have a huge part to play in what will surely be a vocal and vociferous atmosphere inside Portman Road.

SHEFFIELD UNITED · HOME
SATURDAY 10TH MARCH

Back in the championship, Sheffield United arrive at Portman Road in early spring. With various Play-Off matches and dramatic comebacks over the years, games against the Blades have rarely been dull.

WOLVES · HOME
SATURDAY 27TH JANUARY

Mick McCarthy's former club visit Portman Road in what will be a tough encounter. Having spent big over the last couple of seasons, Wolves fans will expect their team to be challenging at the top of the table and this will be a stern test for the Tractor Boys.

MIDDLESBROUGH · HOME
SUNDAY 6TH MAY

Town's 2017/18 season wraps up at home against one of the promotion favourites. Relegated from the Premier League the previous season, the Boro fans will expect their team to be challenging for a return to the top flight.

THE SECOND HALF OF THE SEASON

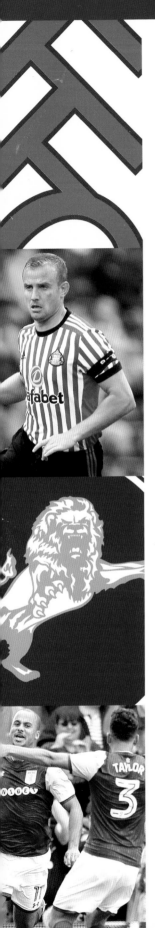

JANUARY 2018

Tuesday	2	Fulham	A	7.45pm
Saturday	**13**	**Leeds United**	**H**	**3.00pm**
Saturday	20	Bolton Wanderers	A	3.00pm
Saturday	**27**	**Wolves**	**H**	**3.00pm**

FEBRUARY 2018

Saturday	3	Sunderland	A	3.00pm
Saturday	**10**	**Burton Albion**	**H**	**3.00pm**
Sunday	18	Norwich City	A	12noon
Tuesday	**20**	**Cardiff City**	**H**	**7.45pm**
Saturday	24	Preston North End	A	3.00pm

MARCH 2018

Saturday	**3**	**Hull City**	**H**	**3.00pm**
Tuesday	6	Sheff Wednesday	A	7.45pm
Saturday	**10**	**Sheffield United**	**H**	**3.00pm**
Saturday	17	Bristol City	A	3.00pm
Saturday	31	Birmingham City	A	3.00pm

APRIL 2018

Monday	**2**	**Millwall**	**H**	**3.00pm**
Saturday	7	Brentford	A	3.00pm
Tuesday	**10**	**Barnsley**	**H**	**7.45pm**
Saturday	14	Nottingham Forest	A	3.00pm
Saturday	**21**	**Aston Villa**	**H**	**3.00pm**
Saturday	28	Reading	A	3.00pm

MAY 2018

Sunday	**6**	**Middlesbrough**	**H**	**12.30pm**

Andre Dozzell was born in Ipswich on 2 May 1999 and is the son of former Town midfielder Jason who made over 400 appearances for the club across two spells at Portman Road during the 1980s and '90s.

A product of the Blues' youth Academy, Dozzell has been on the club's books since he was just nine years old. He has made his way through the Academy age groups into first team contention and having had a taste of first team football he was certainly hopeful of having a big impact in manager Mick McCarthy's side during the 2017/18 Sky Bet Championship campaign. However, a cruciate ligament injury sustained during Town's 1-0 victory over Birmingham City on the opening day of the season sadly curtailed his immediate progress.

An exciting talent with pace, excellent close control and a real eye for goal, Dozzell's talents have already been recognised by England at youth level and the attacking midfielder has been capped at under-16, under-17, under-18 and under-19 level.

Having been a star performer for Town's Academy under-18 side during his first season as a full-time scholar with the club, Dozzell made his first team debut at the tail end of the 2015/16 season. On Saturday 16 April 2016, Dozzell followed in his father's footsteps by making his Town debut aged just 16 and marking the occasion with a goal. Dozzell replaced Kevin Foley in the half-time interval with Town trailing to a Fernando Forestieri goal and proceeded to score Town's 71st minute equaliser to seal a point from a 1-1 draw against the promotion-chasing Owls.

After making such a positive impact on his first team debut, Dozzell was handed his first start when Town faced Fulham three days later at Portman Road. The occasion was certainly a proud one for both father and son plus the Town's faithful who take great delight as seeing a local talent emerge on the first team scene.

The 2016/17 season saw the club continue to carefully manage Dozzell's development. A regular performer at under-23 level, he also made nine in the first team.

There is clearly a 'new Dozzell in Town' and fans will be hoping to see Andre make a swift recovery from his opening day setback and grace the first team on a regular basis in the future.

MADE IN IPSWICH

JONAS **3**
KNUDSEN

ANSWERS

PAGE 26 · WHO ARE YER?

1. Cole Skuse. 2. Grant Ward. 3. Dominic Iorfa. 4. Flynn Downes.
5. Andre Dozzell. 6. Luke Chambers. 7. Jonas Knudsen.
8. Tommy Smith. 9. Joe Garner. 10. Jordan Spence.

PAGE 31 · FOOTBALL 50

Fixture.

PAGE 38
CHAMPIONSHIP CHALLENGE PART 1

1. John Terry. 2. Bayern Munich. 3. Steve Bruce. 4. Angus MacDonald.
5. Crystal Palace. 6. Paul Heckingbottom. 7. Craig Gardner. 8. 2011.
9. Jota. 10. Four times. 11. Middlesbrough. 12. Phil Parkinson.
13. 4-1. 14. Neal Maupay. 15. Mark Warburton. 16.Tammy Abraham.
17. Watford. 18. Tammy Abraham. 19. Nigel Clough. 20. Liam Boyce.
21. Stephen Warnock. 22. Red. 23. Neil Warnock. 24. Gary Medel.
25. Bradley Johnson. 26. 1946. 27. Tom Huddlestone. 28.Atletico Madrid.
29. Marcus Bettinelli. 30. Tom Cairney. 31. The Tigers. 32. Russia.
33. Arsenal. 34. Joe Garner. 35. Sir Alf Ramsey. 36. 1977/78.

PAGE 40
CHAMPIONSHIP CHALLENGE PART 2

37. Marching On Together. 38. Seven. 39. Liam Cooper.
40. Connor Roberts. 41. Seville. 42. The League Cup. 43. Neil Harris.
44. Manchester United. 45. The Lions. 46. Borussia Dortmund II. 47. Four.
48. Angus Gunn. 49. Newcastle United. 50. True. 51. Liam Bridcutt.
52. Jordan Hugill. 53. David Moyes. 54. Won all four divisions of English
football. 55. Nedum Onuoha. 56. Christopher Samba. 57. Martin O'Neill.
58. Jaap Stam. 59. Third. 60. Vito Mannone. 61. Leon Clarke. 62. 100.
63. Chelsea. 64. George Boyd. 65. 150 years old, they were formed in 1867.
66. 8. 67. Callum McManaman. 68. Three: Aston Villa, Preston North End
and Leeds United. 69. George Honeyman and Lynden Gooch.
70. Southampton. 71. Six, 72. Ruben Neves.

PAGE 44 · WORLD CUP QUIZ

1930 - Argentina. 1934 - Four. 1938 - Paris. 1950 - USA. 1954 - Hungary.
1958 & 1962 - Brazil. 1966 - World Cup Willie. 1970 - Italy.
1974 - The Cruyff turn, after legendary Dutch footballer Johan Cruyff.
1978 - Mario Kempes. 1982 - Paul Mariner. 1986 - Diego Maradona.
1990 - Cameroon. 1994 - Russia. 1998 - Ronaldo.
2002 - Republic of Ireland. 2006 - Portugal 1-0 Netherlands.
2010 - New Zealand. They drew all three of the games.
2014 - Hosts: Brazil. Winners: Germany. 2018 - Russia.

PAGE 56 · HOME TURF

1. West Bromwich Albion, The Hawthorns, 26,852.
2. Birmingham City, St Andrew's Stadium, 29,409.
3. Everton, Goodison Park, 39,572.
4. Arsenal, Emirates Stadium, 60,432.
5. Manchester United, Old Trafford, 75,643.
6. Aston Villa, Villa Park, 42,682.
7. Queens Park Rangers, Loftus Road, 18,439.
8. Sunderland, Stadium of Light, 49,000.
9. Leicester City, King Power Stadium, 32,312.
10. Nottingham Forest, City Ground, 30,445.
11. West Ham United, London Stadium, 57,000.
12. Fulham, Craven Cottage, 25,700.
13. Burnley, Turf Moor, 21,800.
14. Southampton, St Mary's Stadium, 32,505.
15. Stoke City, bet365 Stadium, 27,902.
16. Norwich City, Carrow Road, 27,244.
17. Wolverhampton Wanderers, Molineux Stadium, 31,700.
18. Millwall, The Den, 20,146.
19. Chelsea, Stamford Bridge, 41,663.
20. Derby County, Pride Park Stadium, 33,597.